Words that appear in **bold** type are defined in the glossary on pages 28 and 29.

Please visit our web site at: www.garethstevens.com
For a free color catalog describing Gareth Stevens Publishing's
list of high-quality books and multimedia programs, call
1-800-542-2595 (USA) or 1-800-387-3178 (Canada).
Gareth Stevens Publishing's fax: (414) 332-3567.

Library of Congress Cataloging-in-Publication Data

Baumbusch, Brigitte.
    Birds in art / by Brigitte Baumbusch.
        p. cm. — (What makes a masterpiece?)
    Includes index.
    ISBN 0-8368-4443-2 (lib. bdg.)
     1. Birds in art—Juvenile literature.   I. Title.
  N7665.B38   2005
  704.9′4328—dc22   2004057129

This edition first published in 2005 by
Gareth Stevens Publishing
A WRC Media Company
330 West Olive Street, Suite 100
Milwaukee, Wisconsin 53212 USA

Copyright © Andrea Dué s.r.l. 2003

This U.S. edition copyright © 2005 by Gareth Stevens, Inc.
Additional end matter copyright © 2005 by Gareth Stevens, Inc.

Translator: Erika Pauli

Gareth Stevens series editor: Dorothy L. Gibbs
Gareth Stevens art direction: Tammy West

BIRDS
in Art

by Brigitte Baumbusch

GARETH**STEVENS**
GS PUBLISHING
A WRC Media Company

What makes a bird . . .

A newly hatched bird in a bowl that looks like a nest is the **sculptured** cover of an Egyptian vase. The vase is more than 3,300 years old. The nest and the eggs are carved stone. The bird is made of wood.

A bird and its nest are also featured in this painting from the mid 1900s by French artist Georges Braque.

a masterpiece?

Birds can be paintings...

The birds and plants around the pond in this **Florentine fresco** are painted in precise detail. The fresco is from the mid-fifteenth century. The artist was an Italian **Renaissance** painter named Benozzo Gozzoli.

The sixteenth-century sculptor who made this magnificent **bronze** eagle (above) was from Flanders, which, today, is the country of Belgium. His name was Jean de Boulogne. Although born in Belguim, he lived and worked in Italy, especially in Florence, where he was called Giambologna.

or sculptures.

Some birds are big . . .

This big vase (right) in the shape of an eagle was made in France in the **Middle Ages**, about eight and a half centuries ago. The body of the vase is a dark, **variegated** stone called **porphyry**. The eagle's head and wings are made of **gilded** silver.

and some are . . .

Ducks flock around a barnyard puddle in this painting by Italian artist Giuseppe De Nittis, who lived during the nineteenth century.

little.

Birds can be made of pottery . . .

This water **flask** in shiny black **terra-cotta** has two little birds perched under its handle. It comes from Peru and is five to eight hundred years old.

or ivory . . .

Made about 2,300 years ago in the **ancient** city of Ugarit, which is now in Syria, this duck carved out of ivory was used to hold **cosmetics**.

The parrot pictured above was made in Italy in the seventeenth century, using colored stones in a technique known as **intarsia**.

or colored stones.

Birds can also be made of wood . . .

Fortunato Depero, an Italian artist of the twentieth-century, made this head of a bird out of colored wood. With its simple design, this sculpture looks a lot like a toy.

Birds and plants in mother-of-pearl decorate a lacquer box made in Korea in the nineteenth century.

Mother-of-pearl is the inner layer of a certain kind of seashell that sometimes contains a pearl.

Lacquer is a shiny black **resin** used in China, Japan, and Korea to **varnish** furniture and many other objects made of wood.

or mother-of-pearl.

Sometimes, birds look elegant.

Flying cranes look both
elegant and graceful in
this seventeenth-century
painting by Japanese
artist Tawaraya Sotatsu.

Sometimes, they look . . .

When they are on the
ground, many birds
look far from graceful.
This brightly colored
flamingo is an example.
It was painted in the
nineteenth century by
John James Audubon,
an American artist who
was also a **naturalist**.

awkward.

Some birds . . .

These lively little sparrows in a basket appear to be chirping at the tops of their voices. They were painted on silk in China more than seven centuries ago.

make noise.

The title of this picture by Swiss artist Paul Klee is "The Twittering Machine." It was painted in 1922.

Others sing.

Birds of prey hunt...

Some birds, such as hawks, owls, and eagles, **prey** on other animals. This winter **landscape** shows a hawk hunting a hare. It was painted by Mijo Kovacic, a Yugoslavian folk artist of the twentieth century.

A hunter has killed these two **mallards**, and they will soon be roasted for dinner. This seventeenth-century Italian still life is **trompe l'oeil**, which is an artistic technique that makes painted objects look real. A still life is a picture of objects up close, without people.

while other birds are hunted.

Birds with big tails . . .

Peacocks are famous for their beautiful tail feathers, which they proudly open like huge fans for others to admire.

The peacock below was painted by Russian artist Natalya Goncharova in 1911.

This peacock ornament (above) was made more than three centuries ago, using a pearl for the body.

The peacock to the left is a sixth-century **mosaic** from a church in the Italian city of Ravenna.

are a sight to see.

Birds with big eyes . . .

This mosaic landscape of various birds, made four centuries ago, includes a screech owl with large, staring eyes in the **foreground**. The mosaic uses such tiny stones that it's hard to believe the landscape isn't painted.

In ancient Greece, an owl was the **symbol** of the city of Athens. This coin with an owl on it was used in Athens almost 2,500 years ago.

can see in the dark . . .

Tinwork is still an art form in Mexico. This painted tin owl was made by a Mexican **artisan** not too many years ago.

and fly at night.

Some birds don't fly at all.

Birds such as turkeys, ostriches, emus, and penguins don't know how to fly.

The turkey picture to the left was painted by French artist Claude Monet in 1877.

This pair of walking ostriches was painted on a rock in the Sahara desert more than 11,000 years ago.

These birds are . . .

At one time, small birds were given to children as playthings. This little Italian prince (left) is holding a finch. The child was **portrayed** in the sixteenth century by a Florentine painter named Bronzino.

This mechanical toy bird from the 1950s hops when it is wound up with a key.

just for fun.

GLOSSARY

ancient
relating to a period in history from the earliest civilizations until about the time of the Roman Empire

artisan
a craftsperson; a person who is highly skilled in a handicraft or a trade, such as cabinetmaking or metalwork

bronze
a hard metal alloy (combination of two or more metals) that is a mixture of mainly copper and tin

cosmetics
substances used, especially on the face, to improve or beautify skin; makeup

flask
a container for carrying liquids, which typically has a narrow neck that can be closed with a cap or a stopper to prevent spilling

Florentine
related to the area of northern Italy in and around the city of Florence

foreground
the part of a picture or scene that is closest to the front or nearest the viewer

fresco
a painting on a wall; specifically, a type of painting that is typically done on fresh, damp plaster, using water-based paints or coloring

gilded
covered with a thin layer of a metallic gold or silver coating

intarsia
the process of making a design or a picture by gluing small, thin pieces of wood, ivory, marble, mother-of-pearl, or other artistic materials into place within some kind of sturdy frame

landscape
a wide view of the natural scenery or landforms of a particular area, seen all at the same time from one place

mallards
wild ducks belonging to a common species of the northern hemisphere, the males of which are easily recognized by their dark green heads and the white ring around the bottom of their necks

Middle Ages
a period of history in Europe from the end of the Roman Empire to the 1500s

mosaic
a scene or design made by arranging small, irregularly shaped pieces of materials such as stone, glass, tile, or wood in glue, plaster, or some other kind of surface material that holds the pieces securely in place

naturalist
a person who has a strong, active interest in natural history and studies animals and plants in their natural environments

porphyry
a type of rock that is dark red or purple with flecks of crystal in it

portrayed
pictured, especially in the style of a portrait, with just the head, neck, and shoulders or partial upper body showing

prey
(v) to hunt and kill for food

Renaissance
a period of European history, between the Middle Ages (14th century) and modern times (17th century), during which learning flourished and interest in classical (relating to ancient Greek and Roman civilizations) art and literature was renewed, or "reborn"

resin
a natural or chemically manufactured substance which, because it does not dissolve in water, is a common ingredient in plastics, varnishes, and printing inks

sculptured
made by carving, modeling, or molding materials such as wood, rock, stone, or clay

symbol
an object or figure that stands for or represents something else

terra-cotta
brownish-orange earth, or clay, that hardens when it is baked and is often used to make pottery and roofing tiles

trompe l'oeil
a French term meaning "fool the eye" that describes a style of painting in which subjects are depicted in such a lifelike way that they are often seen as the real thing

variegated
having a variety of different colors

varnish
(v) to cover with a usually transparent liquid coating that dries to form a hard, and often shiny, protective surface

PICTURE LIST

page 4 – Bird's nest with eggs and a newly hatched chick, cover of a vase in calcite and painted wood. Egyptian art, XIX dynasty, c. 1330 B.C., from the tomb of Tutankhamon. Cairo, Egyptian Museum. Drawing by Sauro Giampaia.

page 5 – Georges Braque (1882-1963): The Bird and Its Nest, 1956. Paris, Musée National d'Art Moderne. Photo Scala Archives. © Georges Braque by SIAE, 2003.

pages 6-7 – Benozzo Gozzoli (1420-1497): Detail of a pond with birds, from the fresco cycle with the Procession of the Magi. Florence, Chapel of the Medici, Riccardi Palace. Photo Scala Archives.

page 7 – Giambologna (1529-1608): Bronze eagle. Florence, Bargello Museum. Photo Scala Archives.

pages 8-9 – Giuseppe De Nittis (1846-1884): Ducks. Florence, Gallery of Modern Art. Photo Scala Archives.

page 9 – Eagle-shaped vase known as "Suger's Eagle," in porphyry and gilded silver. Medieval French art of the mid-12th century, from the Treasury of Saint-Denis. Paris, Louvre. Photo Scala Archives.

page 10 – Black terra-cotta flask with two small birds. Chimú culture, Peru,

12th to 15th centuries A.D. Barcelona, Museo Barbier-Mueller. Drawing by Sauro Giampaia.

Duck-shaped ivory cosmetic case. Phoenician art, 13th century B.C., from Ugarit (Ras-Shamra, Syria). Paris, Louvre. Photo RMN.

page 11 – Parrot on a branch, inlay in semiprecious stones. Italian art of the 17th century. Florence, Opificio delle Pietre Dure. Photo Scala Archives.

page 12 – Fortunato Depero (1892-1960): Parrot in wood, 1916. Orosei (Sardinia), Museo Nanni Guiso. Photo Aurelio Amendola. © Fortunato Depero by SIAE, 2003.

page 13 – Birds among branches, mother-of-pearl inlay on a lacquer box. 19th-century Korean art. Newark, Newark Museum. Photo Art Resource / Scala.

pages 14-15 – Tawaraya Sotatsu (early 17th century): Flock of cranes in flight, from an anthology of the calligraphist Hon-ami Koetsu. Kyoto, National Museum. Drawing by Sauro Giampaia.

page 15 – John James Audubon (1785-1851): American flamingo. Philadelphia, Free Library. Photo Scala Archives.

page 16 – Song Rozhi (13th century): Young Sparrows in a Basket. Tokyo, National Museum. Drawing by Sauro Giampaia.

page 17 – Paul Klee (1879-1940): The Twittering Machine, 1922. New York, Museum of Modern Art. Photo Museum of Modern Art / Scala 2003. © Paul Klee by SIAE, 2003.

page 18 – Mijo Kovacic (20th century): Sparrow hawk, 1962. Zagabria, Gallery of Modern Art. Photo Scala Archives.

page 19 – Cesare Dandini (1595-1658): Two mallards strung up. Florence, Uffizi. Photo Scala Archives.

page 20 – Natalya Goncharova (1881-1962): Peacock under a Bright Sun, 1911. Moscow, Tretyakov Gallery. Photo G. Westermann / Artothek. © Natalya Goncharova by SIAE, 2003.

page 21 – Peacock, small tabletop ornament in pearl and enamels. Florentine art of the late 17th to early 18th centuries. Florence, Museo degli Argenti. Photo Scala Archives.

Peacock, detail of the mosaic decoration in the presbytery. Byzantine art of the mid 6th century. Ravenna, Church of San Vitale. Photo Scala Archives.

page 22 – Marcello Provenzale (1575-1639): Landscape with birds, mosaic. Florence, Museo degli Argenti. Photo Scala Archives.

page 23 – Reverse of a silver Attic coin with owl. Greek art, 5th century B.C. Paris, Cabinet des Médailles. Drawing by Sauro Giampaia.

Ramón Fosado (20th century): Colored tin owl. Private property. Drawing by Sauro Giampaia.

page 24 – Claude Monet (1840-1926): The Turkeys, 1877. Paris, Musée d'Orsay. Photo Scala Archives.

page 25 – Two ostriches. Prehistoric rock art, 10th millennium B.C. Asadjan Oua Mellen (Algeria). After a copy by Jolantha Tschudi. Drawing by Sauro Giampaia.

page 26 – Bronzino (1503-1572): Portrait of Garcia de' Medici. Florence, Uffizi. Photo Scala Archives.

page 27 – Little bird, mechanical toy of the 1950s. Yokohama, Teruhisa Kitahara Tin Toy Museum. Drawing by Sauro Giampaia.

INDEX